SandCastle™

Math Made Fun

I Know about Money, It's So Funny!

Tracy Kompelien

Consulting Editors, Diane Craig, M.A./Reading Specialist
and Susan Kosel, M.A. Education

ABDO
Publishing Company

Published by ABDO Publishing Company, 4940 Viking Drive, Edina, Minnesota 55435.

Printed in the United States.

Credits
Edited by: Pam Price
Curriculum Coordinator: Nancy Tuminelly
Cover and Interior Design and Production: Mighty Media
Photo Credits: Brand X Pictures, ShutterStock, Wewerka Photography

Library of Congress Cataloging-in-Publication Data

Kompelien, Tracy, 1975-
   I know about money, it's so funny! / Tracy Kompelien.
      p. cm. -- (Math made fun)
   ISBN 10 1-59928-527-4 (hardcover)
   ISBN 10 1-59928-528-2 (paperback)

   ISBN 13 978-1-59928-527-6 (hardcover)
   ISBN 13 978-1-59928-528-3 (paperback)
   1. Mathematics--Juvenile literature. 2. Addition--Juvenile literature. 3. Counting--Juvenile literature.
   4. Coins, American--Juvenile literature. 5. Money--United States--Juvenile literature. I. Title.

   QA40.5.K66 2006
   513.2'11--dc22

                                                                                    2006021567

SandCastle Level: Transitional

SandCastle™ books are created by a professional team of educators, reading specialists, and content developers around five essential components—phonemic awareness, phonics, vocabulary, text comprehension, and fluency—to assist young readers as they develop reading skills and strategies and increase their general knowledge. All books are written, reviewed, and leveled for guided reading, early reading intervention, and Accelerated Reader® programs for use in shared, guided, and independent reading and writing activities to support a balanced approach to literacy instruction. The SandCastle™ series has four levels that correspond to early literacy development. The levels help teachers and parents select appropriate books for young readers.

Emerging Readers   **Beginning Readers**   **Transitional Readers**   **Fluent Readers**
(no flags)   (1 flag)   (2 flags)   (3 flags)

These levels are meant only as a guide. All levels are subject to change.

A coin

is a form of money
made out of metal.

Words used
to describe coins:

cent	nickel
change	penny
dime	quarter
half-dollar	

These are coins. We use

 to buy things.

Coins are also called change.

This is a penny. I collect in a big.

A penny is worth one cent. One cent can also be written 1¢.

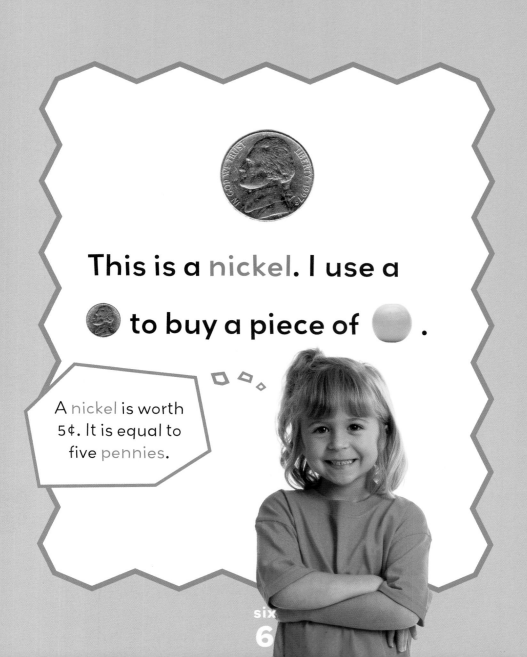

This is a nickel. I use a 🪙 to buy a piece of ⚪ .

A nickel is worth 5¢. It is equal to five pennies.

This is a dime. I use a

 to buy a piece of 🍬.

A dime is worth 10¢. It is equal to two nickels or ten pennies.

This is a quarter. I use a  to buy a .

A quarter is worth 25¢. It is equal to five nickels.

This is a **half-dollar**.

I use a to buy an .

A **half-dollar** is worth 50¢. It is equal to two **quarters** or five **dimes**.

I Know about Money, It's So Funny!

Pete is hungry and wants to buy a treat. He asks the store clerk, "What is the cost of something to eat?"

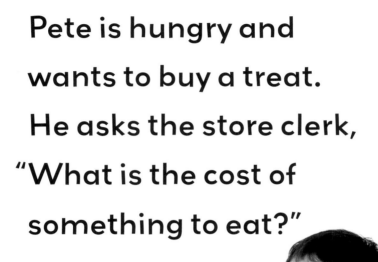

The clerk replies,
"For 50 cents, you can
get a basket of fries."

fourteen

14

Pete empties his pockets
next to the pickles.
He has one quarter, one
dime, and three nickels.
Although it is tough,
Pete adds up his coins.
He has just enough!

Coins
Every Day!

Sara has three coins
and Sam has one.
But they each have 25¢.

I know this
because two dimes
plus one nickel
equals 25 cents,
and a quarter is
worth 25¢.

eighteen
18

I get an allowance of 50¢ each week. I save my coins in a piggy bank.

Some of the ways to make 50¢ are
- 2 quarters
- 5 dimes
- 10 nickels

The jelly beans are five cents. I want two handfuls, so I need 10¢.

Some of the ways to make 10¢ are
- 10 pennies
- 2 nickels
- 1 dime

What coin do you need to buy a ball from this machine?

Glossary

allowance – an amount of money given to someone on a regular basis.

clerk – someone who works in a store.

empty – to take everything out of something.

equal – having exactly the same size or amount.

tough – hard or difficult to do.

treat – something special.

worth – equal in value to.